The Ultimate Couples Quiz Book

By Steve & Kate Haywood

Copyright © 2022 Steve & Kate Haywood

All rights reserved.

Table of Contents

Introduction 7

When We First Met 9

Knowing the Basics 10

Goals Here & Now 11

Top 3... Films...12

Would You Rather? 13

Our Favourite Foods 14

Who's Closest? 17

Famous Real Couples 19

Goals for the Next Month 22

Romantic Holiday Destinations 23

Travel & Holidays 25

Your Next Holidays 27

A Little Old Chronology 29

A Little New Chronology 29

True or False 31

Henry VIII and His Wives 33

Our Goals for the Year Ahead 35

A Few of Our Favourite Things 36

Romantic Film Couples 37

Movie Bucket List 39

Art Time! 40

Wakey Wakey!...42

Famous TV Couples..43

Glad Rags Quiz 45

Our Best Qualities 47

It's a Dilemma..48

Friends & Family..50

Longest Hollywood Marriages...51

Write Your Own Love Poem...53

Valentine's Day Quiz...55

Our Home & Surroundings...57

More Would You Rather..58

Literary Couples Quiz...59

Our Future Goals...61

Our Future Individual Goals...62

Top 3... Music...63

Love Songs Quiz...65

Our Mixtape...67

Who is Better At..68

Hobbies & interests...69

Even More Would You Rather...70

Ways to Become a Better Partner...71

The Big Issues...72

But What About the Little Things?...73

Big Lottery Win!...74

Anniversary Quiz...75

Echoes of Anniversaries Past...77

Thinking of an anniversary gift...78

Anniversary Gift – Full List...79

Top 3... TV Shows...82

Shakespearean Love Quotes...83

Shopping Habits...85

If My Partner Was a..86

Top 3... People Who Influenced You...87

At the Moment..88

What is Love?...89

The Multi Marriage Quiz...91

Design Your Perfect Date Night In...93

More Dilemmas 94

Bucket List 95

Bucket List Continued... 96

Who is More Likely to... 97

A Hearty Challenge 98

What We Have Learned 99

Your Own Questions 100

A Thought to Finish..101

Introduction

Welcome to The Ultimate Couples Quiz Book. While this is part of our Quizicle Books range, it is a little different to the other quiz books in the series. It does have standard question rounds interspersed throughout, but that is only one part of this book. There are also many rounds of questions that we haven't included answers for, because we don't know the answers! These are questions about you as a couple, testing how well you know each other, as well as thinking through together about what's important to you in your relationship.

Many of the questions in this book can be interpreted and answered how you both like, however there shouldn't be anything that makes you uncomfortable – we've steered away from questions that are too intimate or sensitive. Also, this is intended as a truly inclusive book, and can be enjoyed equally whether you are straight, gay, bi, trans or anything in between. This book is all about getting to know each other better as a couple, spending some quality time together and enjoying the process too.

Quizzes by their very nature are competitive, but with this book feel free to be as competitive or as collaborative as you like. Many of the rounds can be played competitively to see who can get the most points, which of you knows your partner the best and so on, but if you prefer you can work together on the questions without competing. It is entirely up to you, and we've tried not to be prescriptive.

We really do hope you enjoy this book as much as we enjoyed writing it. If you do like it, please consider leaving us a review on Amazon – reviews and ratings really are the lifeblood of self-published books like ours.

Also, if you like the books, do look at the other books we've got available. Visit our website at quiziclebooks.com for more details and to sign up for our newsletter – plus we're offering a **completely FREE subscriber only quiz book** when you sign up. There's also our Facebook page which is a great place to keep up with what we've got going on – just head on over to facebook.com/quiziclebooks.

Happy quizzing!

Kate & Steve

8

When We First Met

Where better to start this quiz book than with where it all began? Have a think about your first meeting that kindled the flame which still burns today. For some couples this first meeting will be obvious, but for others you might have known each other a long time before you actually got together. If that's you, then start off by agreeing what your first meeting was. If you like, you can just freely jot down as much as you can remember, or alternatively, you can answer the questions below. Give yourselves a couple of minutes, and either work on it together, or answer the questions separately and compare notes. See who remembers the most, and whether you agree on the details or not! Feel free to extend the time period for this to cover the first day, first weekend or first week you were together, whatever works best for you.

1. First words – what are the first things you said to each other? If you can't remember that, what can you remember that stands out from your first meeting?

2. Who else was there – were you with friends, family members, colleagues or anyone else? Are you still in touch with them, or are they long forgotten? Does someone deserve a special mention for bringing you together?

3. Food & Drink – What did you eat or drink at that first meeting, or in those first days together. Did one of you cook a meal for the other, if so what was it like?

4. First impressions – what did you first notice about your partner, what attracted you to them, what intrigued you? It doesn't have to be something good, was there something not so good which you changed your mind about later?

5. Anything else – if you've got any other strong memories or impressions, or perhaps strange details from that first meeting, jot them down.

Knowing the Basics

You probably know a lot about each other, but how well do you know the basics about your partner? These are the sorts of things that can really catch us out, and even couples who have been together for decades can get some wrong. How will you do, and which of you will come out on top?

1. What colour are their eyes?

2. Do they wear glasses or contact lenses? If so, are they long sighted or short sighted, and what type of glasses/lenses do they wear?

3. What is their favourite colour?

4. What is their shoe size?

5. What size clothes are they, e.g. trousers, shirt, tops, underwear? Very useful to know for buying presents!

6. What place were they born in?

7. What is/was their mother's maiden name

8. What date is their birthday? You really should know this, shame on you if you don't!

9. Are they on the organ donor register?

10. What's their mobile phone number (yes, it is probably stored in your phone, but what if you lose your phone?)

Goals Here & Now

It is good to have goals or objectives, even very short-term ones. What would you like to do together in the next week? It can be something you want to achieve together but it doesn't have to be. It could be as simple as catching a coffee when you've both got nothing else on and enjoying each other's company. Jot down here at least three things you'd like to do together, then check back at the end of the week to see if you managed it.

♥

♥

♥

Top 3... Films

How well do you know what your partner likes? In this case, we're asking about your partner's film preferences. What would they say are their top 3 favourite films of all time? A tough question, and even if you have been together for ever, their answers might surprise you. Here you each get to answer what your top 3 are and see how many matches you get.

Partner A:

Film 1:

Film 2:

Film 3:

Partner B

Film 1:

Film 2:

Film 3:

Were your partner's answers what you expected and did you get them all right?

Would You Rather?

A classic parlour game, this round asks a series of what are deceptively simple questions – would you rather one option or the other? Only two answers, but do you agree? You can either guess what your partner would choose and see if you're right, or just answer together and see if you agree.

♥ Have a maid to clean your house weekly or an hour's massage weekly

♥ To never be able to go out when it is light or never be able to go out when it is dark

♥ Be only able to watch romance movies or only able to watch horror movies

♥ Be average at something people respect or the best at something no one takes seriously

♥ Go to the past and meet your ancestors or to the future and meet later generations of your family

Our Favourite Foods

Food has always been associated with love and romance whether going out for that first date to a restaurant, cooking food for one another or buying chocolates for your lover on Valentines Day. The course of love – and of food in relationships – isn't always a smooth one though. Do you and your partner share the same tastes, and do you know what your partner likes best? Here is a selection of food related questions to help you find out. Some are multiple choice, others you are free to give whatever answer you want.

1. You are going for a romantic dinner at a restaurant. Would your partner prefer:
    a. Just a main course
    b. A starter and a main course
    c. A main course and pudding
    d. Three courses, obviously!
    e. To miss out the main and go with the good stuff

2. You decide to order a takeaway one evening. If it was just your partner's choice, what would they pick:
    a. Fish & chips
    b. Chinese
    c. Pizza/burger/kebab
    d. A curry
    e. Something else (if so, what?)

3. Your partner sends you a text to let you know they're on their way home for lunch and could you make them a sandwich. You've got all the ingredients you could need, what sandwich do you make them? Think about the choice of bread, filling, salad, sauce etc.

4. What is your most memorable meal together?

5. You've stayed overnight in a hotel and are going down for breakfast, It is a buffet with everything you could want. What does your partner choose?
    a. Cooked breakfast
    b. Croissant/pastries
    c. Cereal
    d. Toast
    e. Pancakes
    f. Something else

6. What is your partner like when they're drunk?
    a. Sleepy
    b. Flirty
    c. Loud
    d. Moody
    e. Something else
    f. They're never drunk

7. What is your favourite meal your partner cooks for you?

8. What is your partner's favourite snack?
    a. Chocolate
    b. Crisps/chips
    c. Something healthy
    d. Fried food
    e. They don't snack

9. You go out for a meal, which of these happens most often?
    a. You order the same meal
    b. Your partner waits for you to order before choosing
    c. You have different meals and share
    d. You have different meals, but end up swapping
    e. You have different meals but one of you is jealous of what the other ordered

f. You have different meals and are happy with your own!

10. You win a romantic weekend away in a log cabin in the mountains. When you get there, there's a barbecue and you need to cook your own food. Which of you does which jobs?
    a. Decides what food to have and buys it from the local shop
    b. Sets & lights the fire
    c. Prepares the food
    d. Lays the table
    e. Cooks food on the BBQ
    f. Washes up and clears away
    g. Cleans out the barbecue the next day

Who's Closest?

Time for a little competitiveness now, but just a smidgeon. Here are five questions where all the answers are numbers. You probably won't get them right as they are quite specific but have a guess and see who is closest!

1. How many American households buy a Valentine's Day present for a pet?

2. In what year was the first heart shaped box of chocolates created for sale?

3. In what year was Romeo and Juliet originally published?

4. How many Valentine's Day cards are sent annually worldwide?

5. *My Funny Valentine* is a show tune from which year?

6. How many red roses are given on Valentine's Day?

Answers – Who's Closest

1. Around 27.6 million

2. 1861 – produced by Richard Cadbury for Valentine's Day

3. 1597

4. Around 1 billion

5. 1937 – for the show Babes in Arms which ran for 289 performances on Broadway

6. 250 million

How did you do? Hopefully this stimulated some healthy competition and discussion!

Famous Real Couples

It is trivia time now, so cuddle up, put your heads together and see if you can answer these quiz questions together. We've given you the name of one half of a famous couple – can you name the other person in the relationship?

1. Beyonce

2. Portia de Rossi

3. John F. Kennedy

4. Elton John

5. Kurt Russell

6. Barak Obama

7. Tom Daley

8. Harrison Ford

9. David Beckham

10. Sarah Jessica Parker

11. Catherine Zeta-Jones

12. Prince William, Duke of Cambridge

Answers – Famous Real Couples

1. Jay-Z

2. Ellen DeGeneres

3. Jackie Kennedy (Jacqueline Onassis)

4. David Furnish

5. Goldie Hawn

6. Michelle Obama

7. Dustin Lance Black

8. Calista Flockhart

9. Victoria Beckham

10. Matthew Broderick

11. Michael Douglas

12. Catherine, Duchess of Cambridge (Kate Middleton)

"Love has nothing to do with what you expect to get — only with what you are expecting to give — which is everything."

Katharine Hepburn

Goals for the Next Month

Earlier in the book you looked together at goals for the coming week. Now we're looking a bit further ahead at the next month, which gives you time to plan a little more. Think about anything you want to achieve, or perhaps activities you fancy having a go at. Jot down here at least three things you'd like to do together, then check back after a month to see if you managed it.

♥

♥

♥

Romantic Holiday Destinations

According to a popular website, these are some of the most romantic places to go on holiday with your loved one. Can you identify the place from the description?

1. A 115 island archipelago on the Indian Ocean, this country has gorgeous scenery. Volcanic boulders and lush jungle give way to luxurious beaches and warm water. Mahé is the second largest island with hotels, restaurants and excellent shopping.

2. The captivating blue domes of the buildings on this island are a rare treat to enjoy. See beautiful sunsets from the town of Oia and take a dip in the Aegean Sea, which surrounds the impressive whitewashed buildings.

3. The most romantic city in the world. You can stand at the top of an iconic tower, cross many bridges or enjoy world-famous gastronomy. The Louvre Museum with 35,000 artworks is truly a top attraction.

4. This is a series of tiny islands connected by canals and bridges. Enjoy the Rialto Bridge or take a punt on a gondola. St Mark's Square offers a unique style with plenty of opportunities to shop.

5. A country in Asia, this place is in fact a series of 26 micro islands with a capital called Male. With white sand beaches, exotic food and true relaxation, this is a luxury destination. A very popular honeymoon location in the winter.

6. This location in the USA is a series of islands, but many people head to the capital, Honolulu. The Waikiki area is great for dining and shopping as well as evening entertainment. Experience great beaches full of towering palms.

7. This area is a province of Indonesia that offers a little bit of everything for couples. From jungle to rainforest, enjoy natural beauty everywhere. Make sure you catch Uluwatu Hindu Temple for its breath-taking cliff-top views.

8. Part of Chile, this is the capital city. It is a compact metropolis with the stunning Plaza de Armas as a must-see location. Views of the Andes Mountains and Chilean coast offer impressive views. Hire a car and use this as a base.

Answers – Romantic Holiday Destinations

1. The Seychelles

2. Santorini

3. Paris

4. Venice

5. The Maldives

6. Hawaii

7. Bali

8. Santiago

Travel & Holidays

Travelling and going on holiday is usually what we do together to escape from work and the humdrum of daily life. It's supposed to be fun, adventurous, exciting or relaxing, depending on what type of holiday you like, though of course it doesn't always work out that way. How well do you know your partner's holiday preferences, and do you both have the same idea of what makes a good time?

1. True or False – My partner thinks holidays are all about having an adventure

2. Name three places you think your partner would love to go on holiday.

3. Who does the packing when you're going on holiday?
   a. I do
   b. My partner does
   c. We share the packing
   d. Packing? What's that?

4. What three things does your partner simply *have to* pack for any holiday?

5. You're going on a holiday to a seaside resort. What's the first thing your partner likes to do when you get there?
   a. Get their swimming costume on and jump in the pool/sea
   b. Find a sunbed and get working on that tan
   c. Get the drinks in
   d. Go shopping
   e. Go exploring the local area
   f. Book an excursion with the holiday rep

6. What type of holiday does your partner like best?
   a. Relaxing
   b. Active
   c. A mix of active and relaxing

d. Anywhere as long as they don't have to cook

e. Anywhere as long as there's plenty of drinks

7. Who takes the most photos on holiday?
   a. Me
   b. My partner
   c. We don't do photos

8. You need to take a 300-mile journey across the country to get to your holiday destination. Which method of travel would your partner prefer?
   a. Car
   b. Bus
   c. Train
   d. Flight
   e. Bike

9. After a long flight to your holiday destination, your partner realises horror that their luggage is lost. What would they do?
   a. Panic & get upset
   b. Hang around at the airport even when there's no chance of it turning up that day
   c. Decide its no problem as they'll share yours
   d. Immediately go out shopping to get clothes and other supplies
   e. Head to the bar for a stiff drink

10. What would your partner rely on for their holiday entertainment?
    a. You
    b. Books
    c. Something to listen to music on
    d. iPad or other device to play games and watch videos on
    e. More traditional entertainment
    f. They'd go out to find their own fun

Your Next Holidays

Here's your opportunity to work together to think of holidays you'd both love to go on as a couple. Try and think of three options for each of the following:

<u>Day Trip</u>

Sometimes you can pack a lot into a single day, so what will it be? A whistle-stop tour around as many places as you can fit in, or maybe a single fantastic attraction?

♥

♥

♥

<u>Weekend away</u>

This is for 2 or 3 nights - what will you go for, a mini break in the countryside, a luxurious weekend in a holiday villa or perhaps an action-packed city break?

♥

♥

♥

<u>Longer holiday</u>

Time to go all out and plan that dream holiday.

♥

♥

♥

"Have enough courage to trust love one more time and always one more time."

- Maya Angelou

A Little Old Chronology

Here are three facts that all happened in the distant past. Can you work out together which order they happened in, going oldest to most recent?

- ♥ The first known white wedding gown appeared

- ♥ Mendelssohn's *Wedding March* was first performed

- ♥ The first written use of the word honeymoon was used (clue – it was spelt hony moone)

A Little New Chronology

Here's another set of three events for you to put in chronological order, these are just a bit more recent!

- ♥ The largest ever wedding cake was made

- ♥ The oldest ever bride got married, aged 102

- ♥ The most expensive engagement ring ever was used to propose

Answer – A Little Old Chronology

1. First written use of the word honeymoon (as hony moone) – 1546. According to the Oxford English Dictionary it appeared in John Heywood's *Dialogue Proverbes Eng. Tongue.*

2. The first known white wedding dress was worn – 1559. It was worn by Mary Queen of Scots when she married her first husband. It only became the traditional colour however after Queen Victoria of England wore a white wedding dress when she married Prince Albert. Before this point, brides wore their best dress, not a special new dress.

3. Mendelssohn's Wedding March was first performed – 1842. It was written for a production of A Midsummer Night's Dream.

Answer – A Little New Chronology

1. The oldest ever bride got married – 1991. She was called Minnie Munro, aged 102 from Australia

2. The large ever wedding cake was made – 2004. It was in Connecticut, USA for a wedding showcase

3. The most expensive engagement ring ever was used to propose – 2016. It was given by James Packer to Mariah Carey, and it was worth $10 million

True or False

These should be easy, but can you both agree on whether these statements are true or false?

1. The longest ever recorded marriage was over 90 years
2. The Queen sends a congratulatory card for 50th wedding anniversaries in the UK and Commonwealth
3. The celebration of wedding anniversaries dates to the Roman times
4. According to the film Seven Brides for Seven Brothers, 'they say when you marry in June, you're a bride all your life'.
5. In the United States, couples can get an anniversary greeting from the President for every anniversary from 50 years.
6. A rose is the traditional flower of first wedding anniversaries
7. A chuppah is the name of the canopy that Jewish couples stand under during their wedding ceremony
8. A bedding ceremony was an old-fashioned tradition where friends and family provide a newlywed couple with a brand-new bed
9. Japanese Shinto weddings involve ceremonial sake drinking of three cups three times
10. A Womanless Wedding was type of performance popular in the USA in the 19th century where all roles, including the bride, were played by men

Answers – True or False

1. True - Karam and Kartari Chand's marriage lasted 90 years and 291 days until Karam died on 30th September 2016 in Bradford, England. They married on 11th December 1925.
2. False – she sends a 60th, 65th and 70th congratulatory card and then one each following year
3. False – it is documented in Germanic countries from the 1500s with silver and gold anniversaries
4. True
5. True
6. False – it is a carnation, rose is 15th
7. True
8. False – it was where friends and family put a newlywed couple to bed to establish consummation of the marriage
9. True – also it is in decline as fewer Japanese people get married
10. True – the events often raised money for charities and churches

Henry VIII and His Wives

Henry VIII may not hold the record for the most times married (that accolade belongs to Glynn Wolfe of California, who was married a record 29 times), but he is probably the most famous historical person to have been married multiple times. Here's his six wives, but can you put them in chronological order of when he was married to them?

Anne Boleyn

Anne of Cleeves

Catherine of Aragon

Catherine Howard

Catherine Parr

Jane Seymour

For a bonus point, can you then reorder them according to how long they were married?

Answers – Henry VIII and His Wives

The order he was married to them is as follows:

1. Catherine of Aragon
2. Anne Boleyn
3. Jane Seymour
4. Anne of Cleves
5. Catherine Howard
6. Catherine Parr

Catherine of Aragon was married to Henry the longest by far at 23 years

Catherine Parr at 3 and a half years

Anne Boleyn at almost 3 years

Catherine Howard was a little over 18 months

Jane Seymour was around 17 months

Anne of Cleves 6 months.

Our Goals for the Year Ahead

We've already looked at goals for the next week and month, now is the opportunity to look further ahead – for a whole year! What do you want to do together in the next year? You know the drill by now, get your heads together, have a think and come up with at least three things (though hopefully you'll be able to think of lots more than that!).

♥

♥

♥

A Few of Our Favourite Things

Everyone has favourite things. Whether they are things that conjure up a memory, such as treasured concert tickets or they are a photo or artwork, it is just as relevant. It could be anything that you enjoy having, love seeing or that means something to you.

1) Think of three things that are your favourites in your home – are any the same as each other? Why are they favourites, do they bring forward some special memories or is it about where you got them from or who gave them to you?

2) If your home started to flood and you could not stop it, which sentimental items would your partner save to avoid them being destroyed?
   a) Photographs
   b) Artwork
   c) Holiday mementos
   d) Stuffed toys
   e) Something else

3) One of you has inherited a little money from a distant relative and you have decided to commission an artwork that represents the bond you share. What do you jointly decide to have created for you?
   a) Something to hang on the walls such as paper or fabric
   b) Something small to place on a side table like a wood carving or pottery piece
   c) A metal sculpture to go outside
   d) A piece of glass to enhance a window

4) Sometimes we look back on a period of time, holiday or event and realise that we do not have a memento for it. Perhaps we meant to get one or it has since been lost. What thing do you wish you had from a time that is gone by?

5) You are going on holiday together and each decide to get a trinket for your space. What would you choose?
   a) A tourist magnet, bookmark or tea towel
   b) A piece of stationery such as a pen or pencil
   c) Something from a local artist
   d) A speciality of the local area such as a polished shell or a fan

Romantic Film Couples

Here's another quiz for you to have a go at together. Below is a selection of famous on-screen couples – can you identify the film they featured in? All of the films are romantic films of one sort or another – see how you do.

1. Rose DeWitt Bukater and Jack Dawson

2. Annie Reed and Sam Baldwin

3. Isla Lund and Rick Blaine

4. Vivian Ward and Edward Lewis

5. Ennis Del Mar and Jack Twist

6. Frances 'Baby' Houseman and Johnny Castle

7. Sally Albright and Harry Burns

8. Anastasia Steele and Christian Grey

9. Amy March and Theodore 'Laurie' Laurence

10. Bella Swan and Edward Cullen

11. Mrs de Winter and Maxim de Winter

12. Laura Jesson and Alec Harvey

Answers – Romantic Film Couples

1. Titanic

2. Sleepless in Seattle

3. Casablanca

4. Pretty Woman

5. Brokeback Mountain

6. Dirty Dancing

7. When Harry Met Sally

8. Fifty Shades of Grey

9. Little Women

10. Twilight

11. Rebecca

12. Brief Encounter

How many did you get? Also, how many have you seen? These are all classic films, well worth a watch!

Movie Bucket List

After all that talk about films, here's your opportunity to come up with a joint bucket list of films you'd like to see. These can be new or recent films, films you've seen before or old favourites you want to rewatch together. It might even be films from your Top 3 that your partner's somehow never seen!

1.

2.

3.

4.

5.

6.

7.

8.

9.

10.

Now book in some time to see them – perhaps choose a night of the week that's movie night, dim the lights, grab the popcorn and off you go!

Art Time!

How often do you really look at your partner? By that, I mean really notice them, their features, that dimple on their cheeks, the brightness of their smile? What about their hair, their nose, their chin? This next challenge is meant to be a bit of fun – it doesn't matter if you aren't arty at all, you can go for a basic cartoon or attempt something more lifelike. You can spend a minute on it or an hour… what you've got to do is draw a portrait of your partner. We've included a picture frame for each of you to have a go!

What did you think of the picture? Now it's time for you to have a go (and get your own back?)

Wakey Wakey!

It is the weekend, and you decide not to set an alarm. Assuming you don't wake them, when will your partner wake up?

    a) 7am or earlier
    b) 7am-9am
    c) 9am-10am
    d) 10am-11am
    e) 11am-noon
    f) Afternoon
    g) They won't!

Famous TV Couples

Who is the accepted other half of the character below, to create a well-known television pairing?

1. Kermit

2. Lois Lane

3. Mork

4. Gomez Addams

5. Fred Flintstone

6. Lord Eddard Stark of Winterfell

7. Marge Simpson

8. Aladdin

9. Meredith Grey (father of her children)

10. Tony Stark

Answers – Famous TV Couples

1. Miss Piggy

2. Clark Kent

3. Mindy

4. Morticia Addams

5. Wilma Flintstone

6. Lady Catelyn Stark

7. Homer Simpson

8. Princess Jasmine

9. Derek Shepherd

10. Pepper Potts

Glad Rags Quiz

These ladies all had a seriously impressive gown, but which of their four wedding dresses cost the most? There is a description below which may help.

- ♥ Amal Alamuddin who married George Clooney – it was by Oscar de la Renta and featured in his exhibit at the Museum of Fine Arts. It was the last wedding dress he created before his death.

- ♥ Vera Wang who married Arthur P. Becker – this queen of designs created a dress out of 2,009 male peacock feathers

- ♥ Marie-Chantal Miller who married Prince Pavlos of Greece – it was by Valentino, encrusted with pearls and had a 14-foot Chantilly lace train

- ♥ Victoria Swarovski who married Werner Mürz – as heiress to the multi-billion dollar Swarovski company, it featured over 500,000 Swarovski crystals

Answer – Glad Rags Quiz

Here's how much they all cost:

- ♥ Amal Alamuddin - $380,000
- ♥ Vera Wang - $1.5 million
- ♥ Marie-Chantal Miller - $225,000
- ♥ Victoria Swarovski – estimated at $1 million

So, Vera Wang's cost the most. It is not the most expensive wedding dress ever made, but it is the priciest one from this bunch! It is very much unique and avoids the usual white fabric on show with over 2,000 'eyes'!

Our Best Qualities

What are our best qualities? Is it the ability to compromise, loyalty, love, honesty or something else? List below, firstly what you each think your partner's best qualities are, and then together think about what your best qualities together as a couple are.

<u>Partner A</u>

♥

♥

♥

<u>Partner B</u>

♥

♥

♥

<u>As a Couple</u>

♥

♥

♥

It's a Dilemma

In life, we all face problems to solve and dilemmas that we struggle to decide what to do with, and everyone handles these differently. Here are a few dilemmas for you both. Think about them and discuss – how would you solve them? Do you both agree, or would you take different actions?

♥ It is Thursday and you have been invited to the home of your boss for a meal on Friday night. There is a concert on in your town that you very much wanted to go but the tickets were all sold out. Your friend sends you a text saying their friend is unwell and now they have two spare tickets. You know that several colleagues are going to the concert. What do you do?

♥ You are both having a drink in a hotel where a wedding is happening. As you are leaving, you see a large amount of money in notes at the bottom of a staircase. This is enough to buy a nice overnight trip for you both. No one else is around, what do you do?

♥ You see a car speed off in a supermarket and something falls from the roof and rolls to your feet. It is a plastic carrier bag with a gift inside. It is something that you immediately take to. You look up but the car has zoomed off around the corner and is gone. There is no one around and no obvious way of getting the item back to the person, what would you do with the item?

"Where we love is home — home that our feet may leave, but not our hearts."

- Oliver Wendell Holmes Sr.

Friends & Family

Our friends and family often make us. Here are a few questions about those close to us.

1) Who would your partner say is their favourite member of your family and vice versa? Even if they like everyone, there is probably someone they feel closest to, get on with well or admire – who is it?

2) Everybody's family is different. How would your partner describe your family?
   a) Perfectly normal with one or two characters
   b) Loving and caring but possibly that extends to someone being a bit of a busybody at times
   c) A bit bonkers – lots of eccentricities but it is never a dull moment
   d) The ones they have met are OK, but some have been screened out!
   e) Something else

3) Who are your friends and what does your partner think of them? Choose three of your friends and ask your partner what their opinion is of each one.

4) You go to a new club or event and get talking to some people. Your partner is chatting to one person. They are obviously getting on well. What would your partner do at the end of the conversation?
   a) Say goodbye and forget all about it
   b) Hope to bump into them again at some point
   c) Give them contacts details or a business card and suggest meeting for a coffee
   d) Invite them over to have dinner with you both
   e) Something else

5) It can be easy for friendships to weaken unless both people work at it. This can happen very quickly as you lose a joint hobby perhaps, or slowly as someone moves away. Think about a friendship this might have happened with individually or as a couple. Would you like to make an effort to rekindle the relationship – how will you do this if so?

Longest Hollywood Marriages

Hollywood celebrities are not known for their long and stable marriages, but that is probably because the ones always remarrying are the ones that get all the publicity. A happily married couple is rarely newsworthy. Here are some sets of couples that buck the trend, but can you work out who has been married the longest in each set of three?

Set 1

Julia Roberts (to Daniel Mode)

Cindy Crawford (to Rande Gerber)

Dame Helen Mirren (to Taylor Hackford)

Set 2

Samuel L Jackson (to LaTanya)

Jamie Lee Curtis (to Christopher Guest)

Meryl Streep (to Don Gummer)

Set 3

Will Smith (to Jada Pinkett)

Tom Hanks (to Rita Wilson)

Warren Beatty (to Annette Benning)

Set 4

Ellen De Generes (to Portia De Rossi)

Nicole Kidman (to Keith Urban)

RuPaul (to Georges Le Bar)

Answers – Longest Hollywood Marriages

<u>Answers - Set 1</u>

Dame Helen Mirren to Taylor Hackford (1997)

Cindy Crawford to Rande Gerber (1998)

Julia Roberts to Daniel Mode (2002)

<u>Answers - Set 2</u>

Meryl Streep to Don Gummer (1978)

Samuel L Jackson to LaTanya (1980)

Jamie Lee Curtis to Christopher Guest (1984)

<u>Answers to Set 3</u>

Tom Hanks to Rita Wilson (1988)

Warren Beatty to Annette Benning (1992)

Will Smith to Jada Pinkett (1997)

<u>Answers to Set 4</u>

Nicole Kidman to Keith Urban (2006)

Ellen De Generes to Portia De Rossi (2008)

RuPaul to Georges Le Bar (2017)

Write Your Own Love Poem

Create your very own love poem! Simply fill in the blanks with one or two words of your choice each time to create a romantic/ funny/ silly/ serious poem of your choice. There is one on the next page too, so you can each have a try.

Each day I _____ at your _____

And consider myself to be so _____

From day to day our _____ truly

_____ .

Whenever I _____ you,

I _____ with _____ when I think of you

And all we _____ .

You are truly my _____

And are _____ in my _____ .

Here's the second one, see what you can come up with. You can be romantic, serious, funny or just downright silly, whatever you think your partner would like!

My _____ is forever _____ .

When I _____ all the _____ we share,

I am _____ by you.

My _____ is light when you are _____

Be _____ forever and let us _____ .

Keep me _____

And hope our _____ is always _____

These are re-usable templates, you can come up with a different poem each time, or if it inspires you why not have a go at writing a poem from scratch for your partner?

Valentine's Day Quiz

Here's a few Valentine's Day trivia questions for you to have a go at.

1. The oldest considered Valentine's message was from Charles Duke of Orleans to his wife when he was imprisoned in the Tower of London in 1415, what did it say about Valentines?
    a. I am already sick of love, My very gentle Valentine
    b. I am already sick of pain, My very sweet Valentine
    c. I am already sick of heart, My very beautiful Valentine

2. Love Hearts or Conversation Hearts did not begin as a simple sweet treat– what was its first use?
    a. As a sore throat lozenge
    b. As a vitamin supplement
    c. As a dog treat

3. Valentine's Day is banned in some countries. Which of the pairs below are countries where it is banned?
    a. India and Malawi
    b. Israel and Taiwan
    c. Indonesia and Pakistan

4. In Finland, Valentine's Day is called *ystävänpäivä* – what does this translate to?
    a. Friend's Day
    b. Lover's Day
    c. Sister's Day

5. Why was 1840 a turning point for sending Valentine's cards in England?
    a. The first commercial Valentine's Day card was produced
    b. The first free schools were opened enabling more people to write a card
    c. The first postage stamp was produced at a reduced postage rate

Answers – Valentine's Day Quiz

1. a) I am already sick of love, My very gentle Valentine

2. a) As a medical lozenge for sore throats by Boston pharmacist Oliver Chase

3. c) Indonesia and Pakistan

4. a) Friend's Day

5. c) The first postage stamp was produced at a reduced postage rate

Our Home & Surroundings

1) If you moved house together and there was some outdoor space, what would your partner most like to do with it:
   a. Make it wild to attract birds & bugs
   b. Have a comfy seating area and lots of colourful plants
   c. Make a kitchen garden and veg plot to enhance your meals
   d. Pave it all and make it easy to look after
   e. Something else

2) What is special about your home or the space you share in together? What three things make it unique to you?

3) Your partner's ideal space to live in would be:
   a. A top floor flat in the city to get a superb view
   b. A sprawling three storey house in the suburbs with plenty of nooks and crannies
   c. A smart space in a recently converted factory with all the original fixtures and mod cons
   d. A farmhouse with an Aga and countryside all around
   e. Something else

4) If you could make a change about your home environment, what would it be? Is there something less than ideal that you would choose or something than needs fixing?

5) Where in the world would your partner choose to live if they had a free choice and money was no problem?
   a. In a far-flung destination with something unique to offer
   b. In the place you live now, perhaps with an upgrade of some kind
   c. In the centre of a busy place with lots going on
   d. Off the beaten track somewhere exclusive
   e. Something else

More Would You Rather...

Here's some more Would You Rather questions now, only this time they are a little bit more on the silly side. What's life all about though if not for having a bit of fun?

- ♥ Be a superhero or a millionaire

- ♥ Have giant ears or a giant nose

- ♥ Sleep standing up or work lying down

- ♥ Be in prison for one year or in a coma for five years

- ♥ Build a snowman or a pillow fort

- ♥ Have a mansion in the slums or a caravan in the hills

- ♥ Spend the next week on a pirate ship or at a yoga retreat

Literary Couples Quiz

Can you name the book and author that these literary couples appear in? There's a mixture of old and new books, and some have also appeared on film, which should make them a little easier.

1. Elizabeth Bennet and Fitzwilliam Darcy
2. Katniss Everdeen and Peeta Mellark
3. Henry DeTamble and Clare Abshire
4. Anne Shirley and Gilbert Blythe
5. Clare Randall and Jamie Fraser
6. Charles Ryder and Sebastian Flyte
7. Ron Weasley and Hermione Granger
8. Charles 'Pa' Ingalls and Caroline 'Ma' Ingalls
9. Nancy 'Nan' Astley and Kitty Butler
10. Christine Daaé and The Vicomte Raoul de Chagny
11. Scarlett O'Hara and Rhett Butler
12. Allie Hamilton and Noah Calhoun

Answers – Literary Couples

1. *Pride and Prejudice* by Jane Austen

2. *The Hunger Games Series* by Suzanne Collins

3. *The Time Travelers' Wife* by Audrey Niffenegger

4. *Anne of Green Gables* by L.M. Montgomery

5. *Outlander* by Diana Gabaldon

6. *Brideshead Revisited* by Evelyn Waugh (whether they are a romantic or platonic couple, they are definitely a close pairing)

7. *Harry Potter Series/ Harry Potter and the Deathly Hallows* by J.K.Rowling

8. *Little House on the Prairie* by Laura Ingalls Wilder

9. *Tipping the Velvet* by Sarah Waters

10. *The Phantom of the Opera* by Gaston Leroux

11. *Gone with the Wind* by Margaret Mitchell

12. *The Notebook* by Nicholas Sparks

Our Future Goals

We've already looked at goals for the next week, the next month and the next year. Now look at what your goals are *for the rest of your lives*. Seriously, this is the time to think big, what do you want to achieve with your lives? What do you want to do together? Also think about any individual goals each of you may have, and how you can help your partner achieve their life goals.

<u>Our Goals Together</u>

♥

♥

♥

♥

♥

Our Future Individual Goals

<u>Partner A Goals</u>

- ♥

- ♥

- ♥

Partner B, how can you help your partner achieve these goals?

<u>Partner B Goals</u>

- ♥

- ♥

- ♥

Partner A, how can you help your partner achieve these goals?

Top 3... Music

Here's another Top 3 for you to have a go at. This time it is music. You can choose a song or piece of music, or if you can't decide you can just name a group or singer. Each write below what your top 3 are, then see how many matches you get.

Partner A:

Music choice 1:

Music choice 2:

Music choice 3:

Partner B

Music choice 1:

Music choice 2:

Music choice 3:

Were your partner's answers what you expected, and did you get them all right?

"Lots of people want to ride with you in the limo, but what you want is someone who will take the bus with you when the limo breaks down."

Oprah Winfrey

Love Songs Quiz

Another quiz now and this time it is love songs. Here we've given you the name of the song and the year it was released. Can you name the artist who sang it?

1. Fly Me to The Moon (1964)

2. My Heart Will Go On (1997)

3. I Will Always Love You (1992)

4. Wonderful Tonight (1978)

5. Nothing Compares 2 U (1990)

6. Perfect (2017)

7. (Everything I Do) I Do It for You (1991)

8. Rule the World (2006)

9. Let's Get It On (1973)

10. It Must Have Been Love (1990)

11. Hero (2002)

12. Love Me Tender (1956)

Answers – Love Songs Quiz

1. Frank Sinatra
2. Celine Dion
3. Whitney Houston
4. Eric Clapton
5. Sinead O'Connor
6. Ed Sheeran
7. Bryan Adams
8. Take That
9. Marvin Gaye
10. Roxette
11. Enrique Iglesias
12. Elvis Presley

Our Mixtape

With all this talk about music, now imagine if your relationship was a movie, what would be the soundtrack to the movie? The songs could be special in some way – the song that was on the jukebox when you first met, the first dance at your wedding – or it could be songs where the title or lyrics say something about you and your relationship. Either way, see what you can come up with.

1.

2.

3.

4.

5.

6.

7.

8.

9.

10.

If you're subscribed to a music streaming service, why not create a playlist of the songs?

Who is Better At...

Here's a round that is meant to be a bit of fun, don't take it too seriously or start an argument over it! Who is better at the following things?

1. Sport

2. Choosing where to go on holiday

3. Remembering things

4. Finding things

5. Cooking/ baking

6. Organising/ buying cards and gifts for friends & relatives

7. Making people laugh

8. Kissing

9. Being diplomatic

10. Tidying/ cleaning

11. Looking after pets

12. Driving & dealing with the car

13. Getting up early

14. Gardening/ nature

15. Games of chance where you need a little luck

Hobbies & interests

There is an old adage that says, "those who play together, stay together". You don't have to do everything together, but hobbies and interests can make up a big part of your joint life.

1) What is your partner's favourite hobby or interest? Can you recall the last time they did it and what they most enjoy about it?

2) For your partner's favourite hobby or interest, how do you think they most like to do it:
   a. On their own
   b. With you, as a couple
   c. With friends or family
   d. With people they don't know
   e. Something else

3) If you were going to take up a joint hobby as a couple, then what would it be:
   a. Something sporty
   b. Something relaxing
   c. Something to keep your mind busy
   d. Something outdoorsy
   e. Something else

4) What are your favourite activities or hobbies to do together? Make a note below of three and then have a think. Do you do them too much, too little or just the right amount? Is this something you both agree about?

5) If money were no object, what hobby or activity would you take up? Choose one for yourself and one you could do as a couple. If you do fancy it, then try to define what is holding you back. If it is money, is it possible to put some aside over time to achieve this aim?

Even More Would You Rather

A final set of Would You Rather questions now, so get your thinking caps on and decide which of these options you'd prefer.

- ♥ Go to The Bahamas with your boss or have a staycation with family this year

- ♥ Decide the result of the next election in your country or change the result of the last one

- ♥ Be locked in a room for a month or not be able to go inside for a month

- ♥ Have your partner read all your emails or your text messages

- ♥ Find a priceless treasure in the worst place you can think of or a trinket in your favourite place

- ♥ Eat sardine flavour ice cream or vanilla flavoured sardines

If you enjoyed these questions, why not have a go at making up some interesting 'Would You Rather?' questions for each other?

Ways to Become a Better Partner

This is going to be a tough question for some, because for this you need to take a good look at yourself in the mirror and think about what you are like as a partner. In what way do you think you could be a better partner to your other half? There is the space here for three things each, which is surely plenty to be getting on with, but if you think you can come up with more, feel free!

Partner A

♥

♥

♥

Partner B

♥

♥

♥

Now discuss. Do you agree with each other? Let this open up a discussion about how to be a better partner to each other, and how you can help each other to achieve this.

The Big Issues

Some of the most meaningful discussions you can have together are not necessarily about yourselves, but about the wider world. "Putting the world to rights" is how some people say it. What would you do if you were in charge, joint rulers of the country (or the world)? What 10 things would you do together to change the world?

1.

2.

3.

4.

5.

6.

7.

8.

9.

10.

But What About the Little Things?

After the last round unfortunately we're going to have to bring you back down to earth. You may not be the rulers of the world, but can still do something. There are many issues in the world, from climate change to inequality, racism, sexism, poverty, health, the list is endless. Whatever cause is closest to your hearts, what small things can you do together to make a difference? Make a list together now.

1.

2.

3.

4.

5.

6.

7.

8.

9.

10.

Big Lottery Win!

The last couple of rounds have been very noble and altruistic, haven't they? After that, maybe you just need a big blowout, or perhaps you are inspired to carry on your good deeds. It's up to you, because now it is time to imagine you've bought a lottery ticket together and had a big win (or if you don't gamble, maybe it is an inheritance from a long-lost uncle). Let's say it is $1,000,000 if you are in the US, £1,000,000 in the UK, or whatever your local currency is (if you are reading this from Japan or India, you might want to add a couple of zeros on, otherwise it might not go so far!) Here's a blank space for you to jot down what you'd do with your winnings. Or, on separate pieces of paper you could each write down what you'd spend the money on and see how similar the answers are!

Anniversary Quiz

You may be familiar with the big anniversaries being associated with a particular gift – Silver anniversary after 25 years, Ruby wedding after 40 years, and Gold after 50 years – but did you know that there are gifts associated with every anniversary year from the first onwards? There are various different lists available, but the closest to a standard is the official Hallmark wedding anniversary gifts list which goes all the way up to Diamond for the 60th anniversary. Who know what happens if you get to 61 years!

For a bit of fun, here's a list of clues to various anniversary gifts – together can you work out what they are?

1. 1st anniversary - write a letter or read the news?

2. 5th anniversary – Nature or furniture?

3. 13th anniversary – Net curtains or doilies?

4. 19th anniversary – Girl's name or green stone

5. 21st-24th anniversary – These are on a theme – hot, wet, light, heavy?

6. 26th anniversary – You could spend millions on these, or just make your own for the personalised touch?

7. 27th anniversary – Well they do say it is the food of love

8. 35th anniversary – If you dive for this, better hurry as it may be sadly dying out

9. 37th anniversary – A quiz one, or something more novel?

10. 53rd anniversary – Seriously? Environmental hazard, especially for the oceans and marine life.

Answer – Anniversary Gifts

1. Paper
2. Wood
3. Lace
4. Jade
5. Fire, Water, Air & Stone
6. Art
7. Music
8. Coral
9. Books
10. Plastic

How many did you get?

Echoes of Anniversaries Past

If you are long married or have celebrated many years of anniversaries of getting and being together, take a couple of minutes to see how many anniversary gifts you can remember which you've been bought by your partner. If you haven't had many or any anniversaries, do the same for gifts received on any other occasion. See who can remember the most.

Partner A:

♥

♥

♥

Partner B

♥

♥

♥

Thinking of an anniversary gift

Here's ten more 'official' anniversary gift themes. Take five minutes and see what unusual, interesting or funny gifts you can come up with to fit each theme!

1. Leather (3rd anniversary)

2. Candy or iron – or both! (6th anniversary)

3. Wool or copper (7th anniversary)

4. Steel (11th anniversary)

5. Tools (29th anniversary)

6. Antiques (36th anniversary)

7. Luck theme (38th anniversary)

8. Office or desk décor (41st anniversary)

9. Home improvement (48th anniversary)

10. Glass (54th anniversary)

Anniversary Gift – Full List

Here's the full anniversary list which you can keep for reference, or just have a chuckle at. Some seem appropriate, some a little ridiculous, though if you get to your 58th wedding anniversary, faith and hope are probably needed to make it much further!

1st Anniversary: Paper

2nd Anniversary: Cotton

3rd Anniversary: Leather

4th Anniversary: Fruit or Flowers

5th Anniversary: Wood

6th Anniversary: Candy or Iron

7th Anniversary: Wool or Copper

8th Anniversary: Pottery or Bronze

9th Anniversary: Willow or Pottery

10th Anniversary: Tin or Aluminum

11th Anniversary: Steel

12th Anniversary: Silk or Linen

13th Anniversary: Lace

14th Anniversary: Gold Jewelry

15th Anniversary: Crystal

16th Anniversary: Coffee or Tea

17th Anniversary: Wine or Spirits

18th Anniversary: Appliances

19th Anniversary: Jade

20th Anniversary: China

21st Anniversary: Fire (theme)

22nd Anniversary: Water (theme)

23rd Anniversary: Air (theme)

24th Anniversary: Stone (theme)

25th Anniversary: Silver

26th Anniversary: Art

27th Anniversary: Music

28th Anniversary: Linens

29th Anniversary: Tools

30th Anniversary: Pearls

31st Anniversary: Travel

32nd Anniversary: Bronze

33rd Anniversary: Iron

34th Anniversary: Food

35th Anniversary: Coral

36th Anniversary: Antiques

37th Anniversary: Books

38th Anniversary: Luck (theme)

39th Anniversary: Laughter (theme)

40th Anniversary: Ruby

41st Anniversary: Office or Desk Decor

42nd Anniversary: Clocks or Watches

43rd Anniversary: Entertainment (theme)

44rd Anniversary: Electronics (theme)

45th Anniversary: Sapphire

46th Anniversary: Games

47th Anniversary: Garden or Plants

48th Anniversary: Home Improvement (theme)

49th Anniversary: Copper

50th Anniversary: Gold

51st Anniversary: Photos or Cameras

52nd Anniversary: Bath or Spa (theme)

53rd Anniversary: Plastic

54th Anniversary: Glass

55th Anniversary: Emerald

56th Anniversary: Day (theme)

57th Anniversary: Night (theme)

58th Anniversary: Faith and Hope (theme)

59th Anniversary: Charity (theme)

60th Anniversary: Diamond

Top 3... TV Shows

Here's another Top 3 for you to have a go at. This time it is TV shows. Who's in charge of the remote control is surely a controversial subject for couples since the dawn of television, or since there were remote controls and more than a single channel! What do you think your partner will say are their three all-time favourite TV shows? Is it one you've watched together, or one that's passed you by? Each write below what your top 3 are and see how many matches you get.

Partner A:

TV Show 1:

TV Show 2:

TV Show 3:

Partner B

TV Show 1:

TV Show 2:

TV Show 3:

Were your partner's answers what you expected and did you get them all right?

Shakespearean Love Quotes

Here are eight quotes from Shakespeare and the names of eight plays. Can you match up the quotes with the names?

1. Sweet, above thought I love thee

2. My love as deep; the more I give to thee, / The more I have, for both are infinite

3. Journeys end in lovers meeting, / Every wise man's son doth know

4. Doubt that the sun doth move; / Doubt truth to be a liar; / But never doubt I love

5. I do love nothing in the world so well as you – is not that strange?

6. The course of true love never did run smooth

7. No sooner met but they looked, no sooner looked but they loved

8. But love is blind

The plays to choose from are:

a. The Merchant of Venice
b. A Midsummer Night's Dream
c. Hamlet
d. Twelfth Night
e. Much Ado About Nothing
f. Troilus and Cressida
g. Romeo and Juliet
h. As You Like It

Answers – Shakespearean Love Quotes

1. Sweet, above thought I love thee – *Troilus and Cressida*

2. My love as deep; the more I give to thee / The more I have, for both are infinite – *Romeo and Juliet*

3. Journeys end in lovers' meeting, / Every wise man's son doth know – *Twelfth Night*

4. Doubt that the sun doth move; / Doubt truth to be a liar; / But never doubt I love – *Hamlet*

5. I do love nothing in the world so well as you – is not that strange? – *Much Ado About Nothing*

6. The course of true love never did run smooth – *A Midsummer Night's Dream*

7. No sooner met but they looked, no sooner looked but they loved – *As You Like It*

8. But love is blind – *The Merchant of Venice*

Shopping Habits

Do you like shopping together, or does one of you like shopping and the other just put up with it? Here are some questions to get you thinking.

1) What kind of shopping does your partner like to do best?
   a. Clothes and accessories
   b. Food
   c. Furniture
   d. Gadgets
   e. Something else

2) You want to buy a new lamp for your space, as the old one is broken and unusable. You will both use this equally. You and your partner go together to find a lamp at a shop you both like. How much of the decision will be yours and how much of the decision will be your partner's?

3) How far is your partner prepared to travel to go to a shop they like to browse for their favourite products?
   a. Half an hour away
   b. An hour away
   c. Further away
   d. No distance, they only browse online
   e. Something else

4) Identify which of you least likes shopping. What trick or method maximises the amount of time that person can be persuaded to spend shopping:
   a. Food – having a meal, or a snack break in the middle
   b. Distraction – give them a task to do such buying a gift for a friend's birthday
   c. Appeasement – stop at some shops they like to go to during the trip
   d. Bribery – promise to get them something, but only at the end
   e. Something else

5) What does your local town or city not have that your partner would like, to make shopping more convenient? Is it the same as for you?

If My Partner Was a...

This round is just for a bit of fun. Each have a go, see what you come up with. Enjoy!

1. If my partner was a vegetable, they would be a ....

2. If my partner was a chocolate bar, they would be a...

3. If my partner was an animal, they would be a...

4. If my partner was a politician, they would be...

5. If my partner was a historic figure, they would be...

6. If my partner was a plant, they would be a...

7. If my partner was a fictional character, they would be...

8. If my partner was a paint colour, they would be...

9. If my partner was a film star, they would be...

10. If my partner was an item of food, they would be...

Top 3... People Who Influenced You

This round should get you thinking and provoke some discussion too. You can guess which three people influenced your partner the most if you like, but this is probably really tricky unless you've had a similar conversation before. So, you might just want to answer for yourselves, and explain why. You each might learn a thing or two about your partner that way. No rules to this but try not to pick your partner (that's cheating), or your parents (too obvious).

Partner A:

1.

2.

3.

Partner B:

1.

2.

3.

At the Moment...

How well do you know what's going on with your partner at the moment?

1. What are they reading at the moment – if they read books, what book are they reading at the moment? If not books, what magazines, newspapers or blogs do they follow currently?

2. What are they listening to at the moment? This could be their favourite songs or artists at the moment, a podcast, audio book or a radio show?

3. What are they watching at the moment – this could be a TV programme they're into, a YouTube channel they follow, or it could be something that's not technological like watching the birds in the garden or even snooping on the neighbours!

4. Work – If they have a job, what's going on in the job currently, what are they working on at the moment? Any gossip about colleagues you can remember, or other information for bonus points? If they don't work, what about any projects they're working on at the moment?

5. Do they have anything on socially in the next week – a lunch date, meeting a friend for a coffee or going to a club or group?

What is Love?

What does love mean to you? Use this page to brainstorm together what love means to you both, individually and as a couple. We've included some shapes to start you off but fill in as much of the page as you like!

"The only thing we never get enough of is love; and the only thing we never give enough of is love."
Henry Miller

The Multi Marriage Quiz

For this mini quiz, below are the names of 5 stars – can you put them in the order of how many times they have been married – correct to 2022, you never know with these guys!

1. Richard Pryor

2. Nicholas Cage

3. Billy Bob Thornton

4. Zsa Zsa Gabor

5. Mickey Rooney

Answers – The Multi Marriage Quiz

The answers are as follows:

Zsa Zsa Gabor – 9 times including Conrad Hilton Sr.

Mickey Rooney – 8 times including Ava Gardner

Richard Pryor – 7 times including two wives twice!

Billy Bob Thornton – 6 times including Angelina Jolie

Nicholas Cage – 5 times including Patricia Arquette and Lisa Marie Presley

Design Your Perfect Date Night In

You can't always go out for a date. However, you can always organize your own date night in, and these can be really fun. On this page, you have the opportunity to plan together here and now your next date night in. Here's some questions to help you plan.

1. What will you eat? Do you prefer cooking a meal together or ordering take out? If cooking together you could always each choose a different course to make, or a couple of dishes if it is something like tapas.

2. What will you drink? Alcohol or not? You could always go for something special like cocktails, or 'mocktails' if you are going alcohol free.

3. Theme – do you want to go for a theme? This could really liven things up. It could be something like 1980s night, historical like medieval banquet or it might be based on a particular country like Japanese or Greek.

4. Entertainment – It is not just about the meal. What other entertainment do you want after finishing your meal? You might just plan to see a film (perhaps linked to the theme if you've gone with a theme night), a game, or you might want to move some furniture, put on some music and dance!

5. Ambience – Is there anything easy you can do to add to the ambience? Candles, mood music or lighting, some pictures or posters you can put up?

More Dilemmas

Here's another few dilemmas for you to ponder over. We've deliberately not given multiple choice options for these, which should encourage you to be creative and to think about what you'd *really* do.

- ♥ You have a friend who you used to have a good relationship with, and you saw each other frequently until recently. However, you haven't been in touch with them for six months and they have not been in touch with you. It is their birthday coming up and you usually get each other a present. They tend to get you something expensive that you don't really want or need. What do you do about their birthday?

- ♥ You are eating lunch in your favourite café. You overhear the waitress telling another customer that times are hard and the owner has lost a lot of business recently. They might have to close. When your food comes, there is a large hair right in the middle and a splash of something red on the side of the plate. What do you do?

- ♥ You are staying in a hotel overnight and as you wait to check in, you hear the people in front of you negotiate a free bottle of champagne for their room as well as a discount on the evening meal. You are celebrating an anniversary – would you say anything to the person checking you in?

Bucket List

What's on your Bucket List? What things do you want to experience or achieve in your life? These can be together or on your own. Here's a list to get you inspired.

Bucket List Ideas	Partner A	Partner B
Visit every continent	☐	☐
Dye your hair a crazy colour	☐	☐
Become fluent in a new language	☐	☐
Climb a mountain	☐	☐
Eat in a Michelin Star restaurant	☐	☐
Go skinny dipping	☐	☐
Be on TV	☐	☐
Learn to play a musical instrument	☐	☐
Ride in a limo	☐	☐
Go vegetarian/vegan for a month or more	☐	☐
Get a tattoo	☐	☐
Run a marathon	☐	☐
See an episode of a TV show live	☐	☐
Set a Guinness World Record	☐	☐
See the Northern Lights	☐	☐
Pan for gold	☐	☐
Go on a cruise	☐	☐

Bucket List Continued...

In case none of the ideas on the previous page took your fancy, here's some space to record your own bucket list ideas.

<u>Partner A</u>

♥

♥

♥

<u>Partner B</u>

♥

♥

♥

Who is More Likely to...

Have a discussion, and see if you can agree on which of you is more likely to do the following:

1. Get out the vacuum cleaner

2. Put their shoes away

3. Change the bedsheets

4. Phone a friend

5. Put on the TV

6. Buy reduced price food

7. Be cold in bed

8. Volunteer to help someone

9. Play a game on their phone

10. Fix a technical computer problem

11. Complain about bad service or food

12. Sleep in late

13. Let their phone die before charging it

14. Skip breakfast

15. Scrub the toilet bowl

A Hearty Challenge

There's now a bit of a competition to do together or individually against the clock – time to get up and go for it.

You need to make a heart shape with the following household items on different surfaces- go! -

- ♥ Coins on a table

- ♥ Toothpaste in a sink

- ♥ Socks on a bed

- ♥ Pencils on the ground outside

- ♥ Honey/jam/Marmite/peanut butter etc on a biscuit or cracker

What We Have Learned

Phew, well we've covered a lot of ground in this quiz book. We hope you've enjoyed it and learned some things about each other. Here's an opportunity to jot down what you've learned about each other that you want to remember.

♥

♥

♥

♥

♥

♥

♥

Your Own Questions

Finally, that's all of our questions done, but during the course of the book, have you thought of any quiz questions or challenges of your own you'd like to ask each other? If so, make a note of them here.

A Thought to Finish

Sonnet 18

Shall I compare thee to a summer's day?
Thou art more lovely and more temperate.
Rough winds do shake the darling buds of May,
And summer's lease hath all too short a date.
Sometime too hot the eye of heaven shines,
And often is his gold complexion dimmed;
And every fair from fair sometime declines,
By chance, or nature's changing course, untrimmed;
But thy eternal summer shall not fade,
Nor lose possession of that fair thou ow'st,
Nor shall death brag thou wand'rest in his shade,
When in eternal lines to Time thou grow'st.
So long as men can breathe, or eyes can see,
So long lives this, and this gives life to thee.

By William Shakespeare

Printed in Great Britain
by Amazon